Jerusalem and Islam: The History and Legacy of the Holy City's Importance
to Muslims

By Charles River Editors

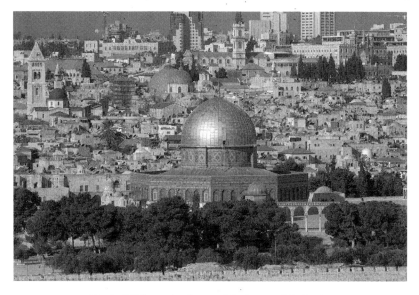

Berthold Werner's picture of the Dome of the Rock

About Charles River Editors

Charles River Editors is a boutique digital publishing company, specializing in bringing history back to life with educational and engaging books on a wide range of topics. Keep up to date with our new and free offerings with this 5 second sign up on our weekly mailing list, and visit Our Kindle Author Page to see other recently published Kindle titles.

We make these books for you and always want to know our readers' opinions, so we encourage you to leave reviews and look forward to publishing new and exciting titles each week.

Introduction

Samarkand, by Andrew Shiva's picture of the Al-Aqsa Mosque

Islam and Jerusalem

"The most holy spot [al-quds] on earth is Syria; the most holy spot in Syria is Palestine; the most holy spot in Palestine is Jerusalem [Bayt al-maqdis]; the most holy spot in Jerusalem is the Mountain; the most holy spot in Jerusalem is the place of worship [al-masjid], and the most holy spot in the place of worship is the Dome" - Thawr ibn Yazid, circa 770

In the campaign leading up to the election of Donald Trump, the Republican presidential candidate frequently discussed the importance of moving the U.S. Embassy from Tel Aviv to Jerusalem. For many conservative Christian Americans and Israelis, this was tantamount to the United States agreeing to Jewish control over Jerusalem. As it stands now, the U.S. has a consulate in Jerusalem, yet no country houses their embassy in Jerusalem due to the conflicting claims of the Israelis and Palestinians. The political issue is just one more reminder of how important Jerusalem is as both a secular and religious flashpoint.

One of the oldest cities in the world, Jerusalem is a holy and special city to the three Abrahamic religions: Judaism, Christianity, and Islam. Throughout its more than 6,000 year history, Jerusalem has been a center of contention, from conflicting clans to warring states. In addition to its religious significance, Jerusalem's strategic location has also made the city desirable throughout history.

While people in the West are more familiar with Jerusalem's importance to Jews and

Christians, Jerusalem's particular importance to the religion of Islam is without question one of the major sticking points in the Israeli-Palestinian conflict. Prior to Israeli control, Jerusalem had been predominantly controlled by Muslim rulers since the 7th century and had been used as a type of political currency, legitimizing the ruling dynasty's claim over the city. This right of control by Muslims was viewed no more differently than control over Mecca and Medina in the Arabian Peninsula. For the world's Muslim population, Jerusalem is a holy site because Muslims believe the Prophet Muhammad visited Jerusalem where he ascended to heaven during the famous "Night Journey." There was also a period of time during the Prophet's life when Muslims prayed in the direction of Jerusalem, as opposed to Mecca. Just as in Judaism and Christianity, Jerusalem plays a central role in End of Days prophecies in Islamic theology.

As a result, Jerusalem has been an important symbol for Muslims for nearly 1,300 years, and it has played a crucial political role throughout the history of Islamic civilization as this important city has passed from ruler to ruler and dynasty to dynasty. Now that the city is again controlled by a Jewish state, Jerusalem has even further implications for various religious groups, and it will certainly affect the conflict-wrought region.

Jerusalem and Islam: The History and Legacy of the Holy City's Importance to Muslims examines the tumultuous history of Jerusalem and its relationship to the Islamic world. Along with pictures depicting important people, places, and events, you will learn about Jerusalem and Islam like never before.

Jerusalem before Islam

Understanding the importance of Jerusalem in Judaism and Christianity is vital to comprehending the position of the city in Islam and the Muslim imagination. Many historians have written about the long history of Jerusalem and its surrounding areas in what is now called the Levant, which is made up of modern-day Syria, Lebanon, Israel, Jordan, and the Palestinian territories. All would agree that control over Jerusalem has been a major point of contention over the last 6,000 years. As with many sub-regions in the Middle East, Jerusalem has had many rulers. Eric H. Cline explained, "It is necessary to remember the turbulence and movement of peoples during the Neo-Assyrian, Neo-Babylonian, and early Roman periods of the first millennium BCE; the coming of Islam in the first millennium CE; the Moslem [sic], Crusader, Mongol, Mamluke, and Ottoman invasions from the ninth to sixteenth centuries CE; and, most recently, the movements of both Jews and Arabs in and out of the area in just the past century. As a result of assimilation, annihilation, and acculturation, it is highly unlikely that anyone living in the area today, whether Palestinians or Israeli, can provide a legitimate pedigree definitively extending back to any of the original inhabitants of the 'land flowing with milk and honey—whether Canaanites, Jebusites, Philistines, or Israelites."[1]

Jerusalem's long history of invasion and transformation symbolizes its current place in the minds of believers from around the world. For the Jewish people, Jerusalem signifies God's promise to deliver His people out of bondage from Egypt to a land of His choosing—Israel, named after Jacob, the son of Joseph. In Hebrew, Israel means "the one who struggles with God." Since the time of King David, the Jewish people have considered Jerusalem the center of their world. The Ark of the Covenant (a large, wooden box that contained the Ten Commandments) was found by David after being lost in a battle. "The king retrieved the old tribal totem, the Ark of the Covenant, and brought it to Jerusalem as the center of a new national cult. The Ark was to link the new institutions of kingship and capital to the older ritual traditions, showing the people that David's monarchy was the legitimate successor to the tribal confederacy."[2]

In the years after that, the city of Jerusalem remained a powerful symbol in the Jewish culture. During the various exiles, returns, temple destructions, rebellions, and expulsions, Jerusalem has called the Jewish people to return to the land they believed God had once promised them. This symbol remained—and still does—in the hearts and minds of the Jewish people as the land of their salvation, proving they are God's chosen people, with a place in this world.

Jerusalem also holds a significant place in Christian religious traditions. While Jerusalem is believed to be the site of Jesus' crucifixion, it is also claimed it will be the site of his eventual Resurrection, when he returns to redeem the world.[3]

---

[1] Eric H. Cline, *Jerusalem Besieged*, p. 35.
[2] Ibid.
[3] Ibid.

Jerusalem and the surrounding towns in the Holy Land also house various sites deemed important during the life of Jesus. Throughout Christian history, Jerusalem played an important role in the minds of Christians in Europe, which fueled the zeal of Crusaders eventually laying siege to the city against its Muslim rulers. Just as it is for many Muslims around the world, the Crusades hold a particular sticking point in the mind of Christians who view the Muslim population as holding Jerusalem captive from its rightful rulers, thus preventing the return of its Jewish population.

In modern times, many Christians believe Jewish control over Jerusalem will help usher in the Rapture and the end of the world. This can be seen in modern Christian groups' support of Jewish control over the city and the encouragement for states to move their embassies to Jerusalem. This, too, is supported by particular Jewish groups in the U.S. and around the world who want the United States to continue to support Israel's right to control the city as the Jewish state's capital. For Jews and Christians, Jerusalem historically belongs to the Jews; the notion that another religious group should control the city—one that came after both Judaism and Christianity no less—makes little sense for many believers.

The Quran and the Religious Significance of Jerusalem to Islam

Jewish and Christian beliefs about Jerusalem are actually important considerations for Muslims. In fact, they also apply similar amounts of significance to some holy sites around the city as do Jews and Christians. In order to better understand Jerusalem's significance in the religion of Islam, it is important to consider its place in the Quran and the Hadith, the main sources of Islamic tradition that Muslims believe guide their lives. According to religious scholar Karen Armstrong, Mecca—the home of the Prophet Muhammad—was a city of merchants wherein people from around the region would visit and pay tribute to their gods, which were housed in the *Ka'aba*. "It was widely believed that Allah, the high god of the Arabian pantheon whose name simply means 'God,' was in fact the deity who was worshipped by the Jews and the Christians."[4] Sources have indicated that many merchants visiting Mecca in the 6th and 7th centuries CE were, in fact, Christians and Jews. It is therefore not unreasonable to assume the Prophet and his followers were familiar with their religious traditions and beliefs.

With this in mind, it should not be surprising to learn that there are many passages in Islamic religious texts (primarily the Quran) that point to respecting Jews and Christians, collectively referred to as "*Ahl al-Kitāb*" ("People of the Book" in Arabic). "Over and over again the Qur'an [sic] insists that the revelation to Muhammad did not cancel out the teachings of previous prophets: Adam, Noah, Abraham, Isaac, Ishmael, Job, Moses, David, Solomon, and Jesus."[5] Instead of claiming to start a new religion, the Prophet reiterated their messages and provided additional guidance for the lives of the believers. Jews and Christians were considered the

---

[4] Karen Armstrong, *Jerusalem*, p. 217.
[5] Ibid.

earliest believers in these messages, but over time, their perception of the messages has become skewed and they were led off-track.

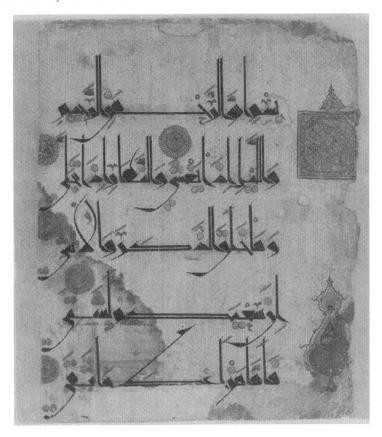

A medieval manuscript depicting the Qur'an

The Quran (sometimes spelled Koran or Qur'an) can be literally translated to "the Recitation" and is Islam's primary religious text. According to Islam, the text of the Quran is the word of God as revealed to the Prophet Muhammad by the angel Gabriel (also referred to as Jibril in Arabic), over a period of 23 years.

\The first revelations occurred at Mount al-Nur, near Mecca, in 610, and the final ones in Medina took place in 632, prior to the Prophet Muhammad's death that same year. In between these two dates–in 620 was an event called the "Night Journey" (known in Arabic as *al-Isra'*). During this event, the Prophet Muhammad traveled on an animal named Buraq, commonly interpreted to be a horse, to a place described as "the farthest mosque" or "the remote mosque," from where he then descended to heaven. This–described in Sura 17 of the Quran–is generally believed to refer to the al-Aqsa Mosque in Jerusalem, although Jerusalem is never mentioned by name in this Sura, or more generally, in the Quran. "Holy is He who took His servant by night from the sacred place of worship [at Makkah] to the remote house of worship [at Jerusalem]—the precincts of which We have blessed, so that We might show him some of Our signs. Surely, it is He who is All Hearing and All Seeing."[6]

This journey is described in more detail in the Hadith, which are prophetic traditions originally transmitted orally, but ultimately written down. These prophetic traditions are accounts of the words and behavior of the Prophet Muhammad, considered essential to understanding the Quran and the Islamic way of life. A Hadith from the Sunan al-Nasa'i collection, narrated by Anas bin Malik–a companion of the Prophet Muhammad–describes a journey to Taibah ("which will be the place of emigration"), Mount Sinai ("where Allah, the Mighty and Sublime, spoke to Musa"[7]) , Bethlehem ("where 'Eisa,[8] peace be upon him, was born"), and then to al-Aqsa Mosque (Beit al-Maqdis) in Jerusalem. The Prophet Muhammad then ascended to heaven, where he spoke with various prophets–including Musa–and the necessity of praying five times per day was determined.[9] It should be noted, however, that some believe the location of ascension for the Night Journey was the Foundation Stone, located in the nearby Dome of the Rock.

Jerusalem is also considered the original direction of prayer for Muslims, which was later changed to the Ka'aba in Mecca. This is described in Sura 2 of the Quran: "The foolish will ask, 'What has made them turn away from their direction of prayer which they used to face?' Say, 'The East and the West belong to God. He guides whom He pleases to the right path.'... We decreed your former prayer direction towards which you used to face only in order that We might make a clear distinction between the Messenger's true followers and those who were to turn their backs on him... So turn your face now towards the Sacred Mosque: and wherever you may be, turn your faces towards it."[10] The "former prayer direction" is Jerusalem, which is also the direction of prayer for the Jewish people.

---

[6] The locations specific in brackets were added to this translation for the reader's understanding and are not originally part of the text of the Quran. The Quran 17:1 (New Delhi: Goodword Books, 2011).
[7] Musome refers to Moses.
[8] 'Eisa refers to Jesus.
[9] Sunan an-Nasa'i, Book 5, Hadith 451, retrieved from http://www.sunnah.com.
[10] The Quran 2:142-145.

The Kaaba in Mecca

Another source of information on this can be found in the Hadith. In a collection compiled by Sahih al-Bukhari, *al-Bara' ibn Azib*, another companion, narrates that "the Prophet (PBUH[11]) prayed facing Bait-ulMaqdis [sic] [i.e., Jerusalem] for sixteen or seventeen months but he wished that his Qibla would be the Ka'ba [at Mecca]".[12] Similarly, the Sunan an-Nasa'i collection also cites al-Bara' ibn Azib having stated that "we prayed toward Bait al-Maqdis [sic] [Jerusalem] with the Messenger of Allah (PBUH) for sixteen or seventeen months—Safwan was not sure—then it was changed to the Qiblah."[13]

There is, in fact, an argument that this was chosen as the original direction in an attempt to encourage Jews to adopt Islam. Some have also argued the direction of prayer had originally pointed toward Jerusalem because the Ka'aba was full of idols and therefore not fit to face. According to Karen Armstrong, the Prophet's encouragement to face Jerusalem was to face solidarity with the Jewish people, and to emphasize that his message was a continuation of their own. It is believed this was one way to appeal to Medina's sizable Jewish population. Such appropriation is common in religion, making it easier for new believers to accept changing

---

[11] PBUH is an acronym for Peace Be Upon Him.
[12] Sahih al-Bukhari, Book 65, Hadith 4486, retrieved from http://www.sunah.com.
[13] Sunan an-Nasa'i, Book 5, Hadith 489, retrieved from http://www.sunnah.com.

religious beliefs and traditions.

As the words and messages of Muhammad spread among tribes across the Arabian Peninsula, the Prophet's personal and political situation with nearby clans grew tenuous, putting the traditional alliance of Jewish clans in a precarious position. Following early battles between the small and nascent Muslim population with clans in the area, many Jewish groups were unable to support the Muslim cause. "Then in January 624, when it became clear that most of the Jews in Yathrib [Medina] would never accept Muhammad, the *ummah* [Muslim community] declared its independence of the older traditions. Muhammad made the congregation turn around and pray fac[ing] Mecca instead."[14]

In order to further solidify Islam's split from previous traditions, the Prophet carried out a variety of measures to break with the past upon receiving further revelations from the Angel Gabriel, directly from God. When Muhammad and the Muslims returned to Mecca, Muhammad immediately destroyed the idols in Ka'aba to purify it from the previous traditions. Upon purification, the Muslims turned their direction to the Ka'aba, which is the current traditional direction of Islamic prayers.

The Al-Aqsa Mosque

Thanks to the aforementioned selections from the Quran and Hadith, the importance of Jerusalem is directly linked to the al-Aqsa Mosque, from where the Prophet Muhammad took his Night Journey. Today, it is situated in the Old City of Jerusalem in modern-day Israel, in an area known as the Temple Mount, or al-Aqsa Mosque Complex. It is considered Islam's third holiest site after Mecca and Medina. Given its age, the mosque has undergone numerous renovations and some reconstruction.

At present, the mosque is about 35,000 square meters (approximately 115,000 square feet), able to hold 5,000 worshipers, and according to architectural historian K.A.C. Creswell who was cited by Amikam Elad, "a fairly large portion of today's al-Aqsa is the fruit of work done during the period of al-Zahir," a Fatimid Sultan who reigned from 1021-1036.[15]

---

[14] Karen Armstrong, *Jerusalem*, p. 222.
[15] Amikam Elad, Midieval Jerusalem and Islamic Worship: Holy Places, Ceremonies, Pilgrimage (Leiden: Brill, 1999), p. 43.

David Shankbone's picture of the mosque

The doors of the Saladin Minbar, installed in the mosque during the time of Saladin

Not far from the al-Aqsa Mosque is the al-Kas ablution fountain, used by Muslim worshippers to perform *Wudu* (sometimes written as *Wudhu*), the ritual washing required before prayer, as well as at other times as dictated by Islamic law. It is intended to purify the individual, as described in Sura 5 of the Quran: "Believers, when you rise to pray, wash your faces and your hands up to the elbows and wipe your heads and [wash] your feet up to the ankles."[16] Initially built in the eighth century under Umayyad rule, it was later enlarged in the fourteenth century.

---

[16] The Quran 5:6.

On the other side of the al-Kas ablution fountain stands another structure, the Dome of the Rock, whose modern-day gold dome and blue walls is an iconic structure known across the world. This building is a mosque that stands over what is referred to as the "Foundation Stone." Jews and Christians believe it to be the location where Abraham brought his son Isaac to be sacrificed according to God's command, was stopped at the last minute, and after which a ram was sacrificed instead.[17] In addition, beneath the Foundation Stone is a cavern known as the "Well of Souls," believed to be the former hiding place of the Ark of the Covenant. Muslims, however, believe Abraham had brought his son, Ishmael, to this spot to be sacrificed, but Ishmael was replaced with a sheep at God's command. In fact, this situation is celebrated in Islam during Eid al-Adha, or "Feast of the Sacrifice." There are also some scholars of Islam who believe the Foundation Stone is the location at which the Prophet Muhammad ascended to heaven. Regardless of whether it is in the Dome of the Rock or the al-Aqsa Mosque itself, it is clear the Temple Mount is a special site for Muslims and Jews alike.

Andrew Shiva's picture of the Dome of the Rock

As is the case with Christianity, Jerusalem is significant for Muslims because of its importance in Islamic eschatology, beliefs about the end of the world and Judgment Day. Christians believe Jesus will return to Jerusalem to usher in the end of the world and fight Satan, the anti-Christ, while Muslims believe Jesus will return to Jerusalem to set the End of Days in motion, destroy

---

[17] Genesis 22:2-17.

Satan, and reign over the world for 40 years.[18] Jesus' second coming is just one sign among many leading up to the Final Judgment, but Jerusalem will play a pivotal role in this scenario. It is believed that the famous battle against the armies of Gog and Magog (stories also told in the Christian and Hebrew texts) would take place in Jerusalem and that they will be defeated by God. The prophets had wanted to be buried there because it was the location of the Resurrection.

It is also believed the Ka'aba will be brought to Jerusalem on the Last Day. "[Jerusalem] was itself a symbol of that struggle for unity, the desire to restore all things to their original perfection by relating everything to the Source."[19] The ideas about Jerusalem's importance in Islam increased when Muslim conquerors took control over the city and had to contend with the previous Jewish and Christian inhabitants, as well as the onslaught of invaders from the region and beyond over several centuries.

The cities of Mecca and Medina are undeniably important to Muslims for a variety of reasons, but Jerusalem holds the distinction of tying Islam to its forbearers of Judaism and Christianity. The Prophet Muhammad told his believers he had not been called upon to start a new religion, but merely to continue what the prophets of Judaism and Christianity had already started. He had also been tasked to bring believers back to the original message of God's oneness and provide guidance to live a virtuous life. The struggle to control Jerusalem since Islam's inception no doubt adds to many Muslims' intensity of belief and further increases their desire to ensure Muslims have access to the holy sites ensconced within its walls. The Muslim belief in the prophets of Judaism and Christianity—Abraham, Isaac, Ishmael, Solomon, David, and Jesus—points to the concern of Jerusalem's protection among believers. Jerusalem is about access as much as it is about religious significance.

Since the inception of Islam in the 7th century and its spread into the Levant and North Africa, Jerusalem's varied religious inhabitants have been forced to live side by side, following the rules of whoever rules the city, implementing their own beliefs with respect to Jerusalem's importance and the ways in which its residents must conduct themselves. Muslim, Christian, and Jewish rulers have shown a preference for particular religions over the centuries, which has, in turn, led to the heightened desires of different entities to control the religious sites. Whoever controls religious sites in Jerusalem could theoretically control the religious behaviors of others in the area, meaning no other city on the planet has had such a long and conflicting history as that of Jerusalem.

Jerusalem Before Ottoman Control

Umar ibn al-Khattab was the second of four caliphs (or leaders chosen following the death of the Prophet Muhammad), reigning during the period commonly known in Islamic belief as that of the "Four Righteous Caliphs." When Muslims conquered Jerusalem in 638, Jerusalem was

---

[18] http://www.oxfordislamicstudies.com/article/opr/t236/e0223?_hi=2&_pos=8#match
[19] Karen Armstrong, *Jerusalem.* P. 242

established as a center for worship due to the importance that had been placed upon the city.

A 19th century depiction of al-Khattab entering Jerusalem

Prior to the establishment of Islam, the location where Muhammad was believed to have begun his Night Journey was the scene of various incidents of destruction and construction. It is known to Jews as the Temple Mount because it is the site of two Jewish temples, the second of which was destroyed in 70 CE by the Romans following the outbreak of a Jewish rebellion. It would not be until around 135 CE, when the Bar Kochba revolt–which broke out in 132 CE–was defeated that Jews were first banned from the Temple Mount by Emperor Hadrian.

There are arguments the Temple Mount had been used as a garbage dump during the Byzantine Period, "in order to fulfill the New Testament prediction that the temple would be totally destroyed." However, other research–based on excavations conducted in the 1930s by British archaeologists–states that evidence of a mosaic floor discovered under the al-Aqsa Mosque dates to the 5th and 7th centuries and bears similarities to churches built in Bethlehem. This suggests a Byzantine church had been constructed on the Temple Mount, which contradicts the idea it had once been used as a garbage dump.[20]

Regardless, when al-Khattab entered the city, he reportedly led cleanup efforts and erected the first mosque, a simple construction able to hold approximately 3,000 people at the southern end

---

[20] F.M. Loewenberg, "Did Jews Abandon the Temple Mount", *Middle East Quarterly* Summer 2013, pp. 38-9.

of the Temple Mount, the location where the al-Aqsa Mosque now stands.[21] Although there are few details with respect to the technical aspects of the building, Guy Le Strange explains in his book, *Palestine Under the Moslems,* that "mosques were, without doubt, constructed of wood and sun-dried bricks, and other such perishable materials."[22]

Reports also indicate that, during this period, Jews were permitted to pray on the Temple Mount.[23] When the Muslims took Jerusalem, they "left the Christians pretty much as they were, but the new Muslim masters of the city seemed to have struck up what appears to be an odd symbiotic relationship with the Jews."[24] It is perhaps worthwhile to note that Islam considers Jews, Christians, and Zoroastrians protected "People of the Book," or *Ahl al-Kitaab,* as they are referred to above. This is because Islam believes the Quran perfects prior revelations from God, first to Abraham and then to subsequent prophets, including Jesus, and finally Muhammad. God (referred to by Muslims as Allah) had previously revealed himself to the Jews and then to the Christians, before providing his final, perfected revelation to Muhammad. Known as *"dhimmis,"* which refers to non-Muslims living in Muslim lands, they are required to pay what is known as the *jizya* tax, which allowed a certain amount of protection, and they were not forced to join the Muslim armies to defend the city against invaders.

The Umayyad Caliphate was founded in 661 by Syrian governor Muawiyah ibn Abi Sufyan in 661 and derives its name from Muawiyah's ancestor, Umayya, who shared descendants with the Prophet Muhammad. It was founded following the First Muslim Civil War (also known as the First Fitnah), which saw Muawiyah fight against Ali, the Prophet Muhammad's son-in-law and the fourth caliph after Uthman ibn Affan–also from Umayya's family tree–was assassinated. Ali's reign saw opposition, including from Muawiyah, who had engaged Ali in warfare that didn't end until 661. In fact, it is this civil war that caused the split between Sunni and Shia within Islam, the latter of which believed Ali and his descendants "were divinely appointed to succeed Muhammad as caliphs."[25]

The main seat of power for the Umayyad Dynasty remained Syria–its place of origin–with Damascus as its capital. Muawiyah and his direct descendants formed the Sufyanid Dynasty, which ruled the largely unified Muslim empire from 661 to 684. His successor, Yazid I, was not recognized by either Abd Allah ibn al-Zubayr–the son of one of the Prophet Muhammad's companions–or Husayn, Ali's son. It would be under Yazid I's reign that Husayn would be killed in the famous Battle of Karbala, located in modern day Iraq.

---

[21] Amikam Elad, Medieval Jerusalem and Islamic Worship: Holy Places, Ceremonies, Pilgrimage (Leiden: Brill, 1999), p. 29.
[22] Guy Le Strange, *Palestine under the Moslems: A description of Syria and the Holy Land from A.D. 650-1500* (New York: Cosimo Classics, 2010) (originally published 1890), p. 90.
[23] Loewenberg, "Did Jews Abandon the Temple Mount", p. 42.
[24] F.E. Peters, Islam: *A Guide for Jews and Christians* (New Jersey: Princeton, 2003), p.228
[25] See, for example, "Fitnah", "Muawiyah I", and "Umayyad Dynasty", *Encyclopedia Britannica,* available at https://www.britannica.com.

Abbas Al-Musavi's famous *Battle of Karbala*

Following Yazid I's death and the succession of his son, Muawiya II, who ruled only until 684, two rival factions emerged, namely, one that supported al-Zubayr and one that backed Marwan ibn al-Hakam, who descended from the Umayya of the Quraysh tribe, the tribe of the Prophet Muhammad. The latter emerged victorious after a battle near Damascus in 684, although al-Zubayr retained control over Mecca while al-Zubayr's brother controlled Iraq. His reign, however, would be short, and following his death in 685, his son, Abd al-Malik ibn Marwan (hereafter "Marwan") became the fifth Umayyad caliph.[26] Both Iraq and Mecca would come under Umayyad control by the end of the 7th century.

Marwan can be credited with various accomplishments, including the establishment of Arabic as the official administrative language. When it came to Jerusalem, although Damascus was the capital, he still pursued construction projects in the holy city. At this time, the aforementioned structure erected by al-Khattab remained unchanged. Marwan renovated the mosque, including its walls, to make it larger and more stable. As opposed to al-Khattab's use of wood and sun-dried bricks, Le Strange explains "it seems probable...[it] made use of the materials which lay to hand in the ruins of the great St. Mary Church of Justinian." The church is believed to have stood in the vicinity of the al-Aqsa Mosque, was constructed in 560, and then "burnt down in 614 by Chosroes II during the great Persian raid through Syria, which laid most of the Christian building of the Holy Land in ruins."[27]

His most notable and well-known endeavor, however, was the Dome of the Rock.[28] According

---

[26] Ibid.
[27] Le Strange, Palestine Under the Moslems, p. 91.

to F.M. Loewenberg, this building was part of his efforts to effectively control the whole Muslim world through economic warfare against his rival al-Zubayr, who ruled Mecca and whose revenue had been almost entirely derived from religious pilgrimage. In other words, Jerusalem and the Dome of the Rock were to be "competing pilgrimage site[s]," with the goal of "siphoning off pilgrims from Mecca."[29]

Conversely, Shelomo Dov Goitein argued against this theory in his 1950 article in "The Historical Background of the Erection of the Dome of the Rock." He asserted that "a thorough study of the sources and a careful weighing of the historical circumstances show that the erection of the Dome of the Rock could not have been intended to divert the Hajj from Mecca to Jerusalem…First of all: the great Muslim historians of the third century, who deal with the conflict between the Umayyads and Ibn Zubair [i.e., al-Zubayr] in the utmost detail, as well as all the earlier geographers, including al-Maqdisi, a native of Jerusalem, never made the slightest allusion to Abd al-Malik's [i.e., Marwan's] alleged intention of making Jerusalem instead of Mecca the center of Islam."[30] Some of the evidence Goitein used to contradict this argument is that parties affiliated with Marwan went on the Hajj. He went on to point out that some evidence used may have, in fact, referred to a custom in which Muslims unable to travel the distance to Mecca went to Jerusalem on pilgrimage instead.[31]

Goitein also cited other reasons for Marwan's construction of the Dome of the Rock, which reportedly "cost him seven years of revenue from Egypt, his richest province." Goitein believed it was intended to rival some of the "gorgeous splendor of the Christian churches of Jerusalem, Lydda, Damascus, Edessa (Urfa), and other towns in Syria" that made an impression upon generations of Muslims growing up in the conquered territory.[32] The Dome of the Rock also likely served as propaganda for Marwan in his continued conflict with al-Zubayr.[33]

Regardless, although the golden dome and brightly colored mosaics were not added until years after its initial construction, the Byzantine architecture, including its octagonal base and its size, makes it one of Jerusalem's most well-known structures. The dome is 65 feet (20 meters) in diameter, its walls are 60 feet (18 meters) wide and 36 feet (11 meters) high.[34]

---

[28] Elad, *Medieval Jerusalem*, p. 24-5.
[29] Loewenberg, "Did Jews Abandon the Temple Mount", p. 42. This theory reportedly originated in J. Goldziher's *Muhammedamische Studies*, as explained in: Shelomo Dov Goitein, "The Historical Background of the Erection of the Dome of the Rock", *Journal of the American Oriental Society* Vol. 70, No. 2 (April-June 1950), pp. 104-8.
[30] Goitein, "The Historical Background", p. 104.
[31] Ibid, p. 105.
[32] Ibid, p. 106.
[33] Ibid.
[34] "Dome of the Rock", *Encyclopaedia Britannica*, https://www.britannica.com/.

The interior of the Dome of the Rock

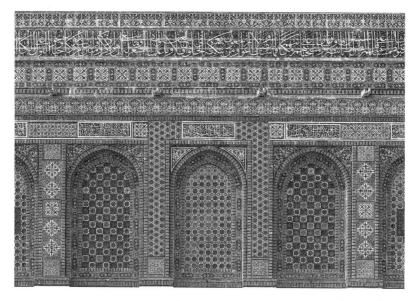

Andrew Shiva's picture of the Dome of the Rock's tiled facade

There appears to be some controversy over the origin and actual purpose of the rock within the Dome of the Rock. Some assert its religious significance to Jews and Muslims while others claim the foundations to have been laid by Greek and Persian conquerors. According to Karen Armstrong, "It is more likely that the Dome of the Rock was an assertion of Muslim identity than it was designed to defect the Hajj from Mecca."[35] There are many instances of similar actions taken by Muslim rulers in the Middle East and beyond when entering a new city full of inhabitants with other religions, such as Cairo, Baghdad, and Istanbul. Again, it is a process of syncretism–which allows for the blending of the old and new religious practices–to assist in the adoption and assimilation of the religion among the local populace. If the invaders had behaved in a manner wholly alien to the current inhabitants, violence and resistance would no doubt mark the change, but Muslim rule in the region—such as in Jerusalem—was rather peaceful, due to syncretic beliefs and traditions.

Along with the Dome of the Rock, Marwan reportedly constructed two gates in Jerusalem, although the location of these gates is controversial. Some believe they were part of the city wall, while others argue they were a part of the al-Aqsa Mosque. In addition, he is also known for repairing roads in the city.[36] Marwan's appointed successor, al-Walid bin Abd al-Malik, who

---

[35] Karen Armstrong, *Jerusalem*.
[36] Elad, *Medieval Jerusalem*, pp. 25-6.

ruled for a short period from 705-715 CE, expanded upon his father's renovations of the al-Aqsa Mosque. For example, documents indicate that, under his rule, construction commenced on three structures, one of which was the al-Aqsa Mosque.[37]

After the fall of the Umayyad Dynasty in the mid-8th century, control of Jerusalem passed to the Abbasid Dynasty, whose seat of power was located in Baghdad, the present day capital of Iraq. In contrast to Umayyad leaders, who have been described as "frequent visitors to Jerusalem," and who constructed palaces for themselves there, the attention of the Abbasids was directed away from the holy city. This was likely primarily due to the distance between Baghdad and Jerusalem, especially compared to the relatively nearby Damascus, the capital of the Umayyads. Some of the Abbasid caliphs, including Harun al-Rashid (the fifth Abbasid caliph) and his son, al-Ma'mun, who ruled during what is considered the dynasty's "golden age," reportedly never so much as visited Jerusalem.[38] Although the second caliph, known as al-Mansur, did make a stop in Jerusalem, he is described as denying requests from the locals to rebuild the al-Aqsa Mosque, which had been badly damaged in an earthquake years earlier. While his successor did ultimately order its reconstruction, he also "insisted that provincial governors subsidize the project themselves,"[39] further demonstrating that at least some of the Abbasid caliphs didn't consider Jerusalem a high priority.

Though al-Ma'mun–e may not have physically visited the holy city, he was responsible for construction projects there, including the replacement of tiles at the Dome of the Rock with new ones bearing his name. At the same time, the situation in Jerusalem, as well as the Muslim population, began its decline under his rule. "During the reign of al-Ma'mun, Jerusalem suffered from famine and became depleted of much of its Muslim population. Subsequent peasant revolts that the Abbasid authorities failed to put down also contributed to demographic decline in the city. In the ninth century, the absence of any strong Abbasid presence led to a deterioration in the security situation in Jerusalem as well as increasing local outbursts against its non-Muslim communities."[40]

At the end of the 10th century, the Abbasid Dynasty was replaced by that of the Fatimids, whose capital was Cairo, which is significantly closer to Jerusalem than Baghdad. The name is a derivative of Fatima and relates to their claim that they are direct descendants of the Prophet Muhammad through his daughter and son-in-law, Fatima and Ali. They also practiced a version of Shi'ism, which saw the Ismaili imams as legitimate heads of an Islamic state, putting them at direct odds with Sunni Abbasids. "Their purpose was not to establish another regional sovereignty but to supersede the Abbasids and to found a new caliphate in their place."[41] This

---

[37] Ibid, p. 26.

[38] Dore Gold, The Fight for Jerusalem: Radical Islam, the West, and the Future of the Holy City (Washington, DC: Regnery Publishing, Inc., 2007), p. 104.

[39] Ibid, p. 105.

[40] Ibid.

[41] "Fatimid Dynasty", Encyclopaedia Britannica, https://www.britannica.com.

brought them into frequent conflict with the Abbasids, including in Jerusalem, which had changed hands multiple times until the Seljuk Turks saw the fall of the Fatimid dynasty in 1071.

During the Fatimid period, the number of Sunni visitors to the city declined and Shia rulers established a study center to spread Shia ideas about Islam which were rather conservative in nature. [42] This was, no doubt, a reaction to Shi'ism being considered an illegitimate interpretation of Islam by Sunni Muslims, and therefore, "the learning there was tended to be conservative and defensive, adopting the most literal interpretation of the Qur'an."[43]

There were instances of clashes between the Shia Muslim rulers and the Christians of Jerusalem as well. At this time, Christians appeared to have been powerful, particularly due to their connection to the larger Christian communities outside of Jerusalem and the Middle East in general. After an instance around Easter involving fire at celebratory festivals, the Fatimid ruler, al-Hakim, ordered Christian churches and religious sites be torn down, and that dhimmi rules be changed to force conversion.[44] This was unusual, but it clearly demonstrates how the Fatimid rulers of the time perceived threats.

During the period of Fatimid rule, an earthquake in 1016 damaged the al-Aqsa Mosque, causing the dome of the Dome of the Rock to collapse. Repairs were made by Caliph Ali az-Zahir in 1022 and 1027.[45] Another earthquake occurred in 1034, but it is not clear if it caused any significant damage.

The prior Muslim rulers of Jerusalem neither barred Christian pilgrims–though an entrance fee was levied–nor were there any concerned efforts to destroy holy places. This changed, however, with the entrance of the Seljuk Turks from Central Asia when they captured Jerusalem in 1071. The Seljuk Turks–the precursors to the Ottoman Empire–had recently converted to mainstream Sunni Islam, meaning that Sunni scholarship and religion had once again become central to Jerusalem's culture. When the Turkish invaders entered Jerusalem they "issued an amnesty for all the people of Jerusalem" and prevented the destruction and looting of the city.[46] In addition to new schools established to teach Shafi'i and Hanafi schools of Islamic law (called *madthabs*), the well-known scholar, Abu Hamid al-Ghazali, who had written *The Revival of Religious Sciences,* spent some time in Jerusalem in 1095, shortly before the city was lost to Muslim rule.

When the Seljuks solidified their control, Sunni scholars and trade returned to the city, and churches and holy sites for the Christians, destroyed during the time of the Fatimids, were rebuilt. There was a period of time right before when the Christian Crusaders had entered Jerusalem that the Seljuks and Fatimids had fought over control of the city. During this time,

[42] Karen Armstrong, *Jerusalem*. P. 258.
[43] Ibid.
[44] Ibid, p. 259.
[45] Le Strange, Palestine under the Moslems, pp. 124-5.
[46] Karen Armstrong, *Jerusalem*, p. 268.

Byzantine Emperor Alexius Comnenus I called on his Western European brethren to save Jerusalem from the Muslims.

After this, Christian pilgrims and churches reportedly came under attack, garnering the attention of Pope Urban II. In 1095, he called for capturing the city from the "infidels," thereby triggering the First Crusade and the goal of establishing Catholic control of the Holy Land.[47] This came at a time when the Byzantine Empire, led by Alexius, was fighting a devastating war with the Seljuk Turks in the Anatolian Peninsula, located in modern day Turkey.

Pope Urban II

Despite its status as one of the major centers of Islamic influence, Jerusalem itself was highly vulnerable. Islamic military and political leaders lacked unity, with many provincial governors

---

[47] Adrian J. Boas, *Jerusalem in the Time of the Crusades* (London: Routledge, 2001).

of Muslim lands refusing to engage the Crusaders, allowing them to continue toward Jerusalem. In addition, factions of Islam were battling against each other as tribal and regional warfare continued between the Seljuk Turks and Fatimids. "We have no contemporary record of the actual words of Urban's speech, but it seems certain that he saw this expedition, which would become known as the First Crusade, as an actual armed pilgrimage, similar to the huge massed pilgrimages which had already made their way to the Holy City three times during the eleventh century."[48] As the hordes of European Catholics made their way to Jerusalem, they took no prisoners and had little mercy for those they encountered—whether Muslim, Christian, or Jew.

Halfway to Jerusalem lay the first large city in the Levant: Antioch. It was also a major biblical city, so it was of great religious significance to the Crusaders. They besieged it on October 20, 1097, but, as Stephen of Blois described it, the size of the city and the impressive nature of its fortifications dismayed the Crusaders, who were now both battle hardened and battle weary and lacked the resources to completely cut it off from outside help. They therefore hoped to take it some easier way, either through treachery or intimidation.

The commander of the city, a former slave of the Seljuq sultan Tutush I named Yaghi-Siyan, was able to call upon help due to a complex series of alliances in the wake of his rebellion against and reconciliation with the sons of his former master. In response, two Muslim relief armies from his allies attempted to reach the city and were defeated. Greatly needed help for the Crusaders came from the west in the form of a naval relief force on March 4, nearly 5 months after the siege had started.

In May, another ally of Yaghi-Siyan attacked with a large army, Kerbogha, the Atabeg of Mosul, was expecting a demoralized and disorganized force along the lines of the People's Crusade, but (like Arslan before him) he encountered a professional, hardened army. And by then, Bohemond had won the city's tower through bribery and the Crusaders had massacred most of the city. According to Ibn Qalanisi, who recounted the story of the fall of Antioch from the Muslim point of view, the commander of the city, Yaghi-Siyan (d.1098), had made a critical error which had seemed like sound military strategy at the time; he had expelled the Byzantine and Armenian Christians as potential traitors but allowed the Syrian Christians to remain. In addition, he had imprisoned the Byzantine patriarch for the city and turned the city's cathedral into a stable. In this case, he appears to have created resentment among the remaining Christians and, ultimately, religious loyalty won out over loyalty to one's commander or city. Bohemond was therefore able to bribe an Armenian in Yaghi-Siyan's guard, a man named Firuz, to betray the city's fortress, allowing the fall of the city. According to Ibn al-Athir, Firuz was an armor-maker who was angry because Yaghi-Siyan had fined him for black-market trading.

---

[48] Karen Armstrong, *Jerusalem*, p. 271.

15th century painting depicting the Siege of Antioch

Medieval manuscript depicting the fall of Antioch

When it became clear the city was lost, Yaghi-Siyan left his son to defend the main fortress and fled with his guard, but he was injured falling from his horse and the guard abandoned him to die. An Armenian discovered him, killed him, and brought his head to Bohemond. With the city now in their hands, the Crusaders had to quickly fortify the city against Kerbogha's advance, but the Crusaders fended him off and soundly defeated him. Dissensions within Kerbogha's army also ensured that it was in disarray in the face of the Christian advance. He returned to Mosul defeated and no longer posed a threat.

The Crusaders had just scored their most important victory to date, but at this point the crusade stalled as political fighting broke out among the leaders, especially between Bohemond and Raymond. Those two had few or no territories back in Europe and therefore were fiercely combative over any territory the Crusaders won and claimed. As a result, the Crusaders remained in Antioch for the rest of the year, and provisioning was so difficult due to the hostility of the local population and the poor organization of any supply lines that some chroniclers claim the Crusaders engaged in cannibalism. The Crusaders were accused of eating local Muslims during the siege of Ma'ara made by the forces of Raymond and Bohemond, a city to the south of Antioch that the Crusaders besieged for two months at the end of the year. Whether this was literally true or a literary device to reduce the Muslims to the level of animals for European readers is unclear. None of the three chroniclers who mention this (Albert of Aix, Fulcher of Chartres and Radulph of Caen) were eyewitnesses. But what is clear is that the crusade was on the point of collapse after a plague swept the city, killing many of the Crusaders, including the papal legate Adhémar.

In early 1099, the Crusaders finally left Antioch and continued south, leaving Bohemond in charge of the city. Bohemond now controlled the northern portion of what would later become the Crusader States, as well as the road back to Anatolia. By early summer, the remaining forces would finally reach Jerusalem.

The Siege of Jerusalem was merely one of several sieges of the ancient city, and it was neither the first nor the last. In fact, the Fatimids in control of Jerusalem had taken it from the Seljuks only the year before the arrival of the Crusaders, and when the First Crusade had begun, the city's inhabitants had no idea that Franks from Western Europe would ever show up at their gates.

On June 7, when the Crusaders arrived before the city gates (following their abortive attempt to capture Arqa in May), its inhabitants knew they were coming. At that time, the city was controlled by the Fatimid governor, Iftikhar al-Dawla, and according to the 13th century chronicler, Syrian Christian bishop Bar-Hebraeus, Al-Dawla answered to the Egyptian caliphate and may have been Nubian or Sudanese. His rather small garrison consisted of Arabs and Nubians, and when he heard the Crusaders were moving out of Antioch and heading for Jerusalem, one of the first things he did was send to Egypt for reinforcements after his attempt to negotiate with the Frankish invaders failed.

A critical decision he also made (according to the 13th century anonymous Syriac Chronicle) was to expel all Christians from the city, though Jews were allowed to remain. Since Christians were the majority of the population at the time, this reduced the civilian population in imminent danger considerably, and it obviously got rid of a population that non-Christians figured could become an internal enemy. While inhabitants of a city were generally expected to participate in the defense of their own home (not least because attacking forces often did not distinguish between friend and foe once walls were breached), it was a common fear that some would choose loyalty to their coreligionists outside the walls instead. Since no sources mention any Christians being killed in the aftermath of the siege, it can be assumed that the expulsion was nearly complete. That said, the *Gesta* does mention Greeks among the clergy who gave a thanksgiving following the siege, indicating some Eastern Christians had remained despite the expulsion.

As a further precaution, Al-Dawla poisoned the majority of wells in the area and brought in all the livestock, two common methods that would make things more difficult for the attacking forces to forage. These were all sensible tactics intended to wear down an army that had already been on the pilgrimage route for years, and the city was well-stocked to resist any siege.

Out of 5,000 Frankish knights and 30,000 footsoldiers in the Princes' Crusade, only 1,500 knights and 12,000 footsoldiers made it to Jerusalem. Repeating their strategy with Antioch, they put the city to siege, but the lack of good water and food made foraging difficult. Both the *Gesta* and Fulcher of Chartres mention an episode of mass cannibalism of the dead following the Siege of Ma'ara in Syria the previous December, underlying the privations of the Frankish army. Now at their ultimate goal, the already-weak Crusaders truly began to starve.

After an attempted assault on the walls failed, the Crusaders took in a few provisions from two Genoese galleys (which were later broken up into siege towers) and foraged wood from Samaria, but it was not enough to prevent their ranks being further decimated by hunger and thirst. The siege was off to a disastrous start.

With things going poorly, a priest named Peter Desiderius conceived of the idea of leading a barefoot procession around the walls on July 8 after claiming he had received a vision from the dead Bishop Adhemar. The idea was to replicate the procession in the Bible that had led to the fall of Jericho; it would last for three days, and nine days after that, the city would fall. He exhorted everyone to fast for three days first, and despite their weakened state, the desperate Crusaders obeyed. The Crusaders concluded the procession on the Mount of Olives, then listened to sermons from former People's Crusade leader Peter the Hermit, Arnulf of Chocques, and the later chronicler Raymond of Aguilers. The inhabitants of the city laughed at them. Throughout this time, the besiegers continued to assault the walls without success.

Following the procession around the city, the Crusaders attacked the walls with siege engines on all sides, and after three days, they were able to breach the walls. They did so with the use of the two siege towers constructed from the Genoese galleys by their crew, led by a merchant named Guglielmo Embriaco. One was manned by Godfrey of Bouillon and his men, while the other was used by Raymond of Toulouse and his men. On the night of July 14, they were rolled up to the wall, and for the first time, the city's inhabitants were alarmed. The *Gesta Francorum* reports that on the morning of July 15th, the Crusaders crossed over at two spots after two Flemish knights, followed by Godfrey and his men, first traversed the walls. Since Raymond's siege engine was initially stuck at a ditch, Godfrey's men breached the wall first, but Raymond was able to turn his mishap into a surrender by the gate near his tower. One account summarized the chain of events: "Both day and night, on the fourth and fifth days of the week, we made a determined attack on the city from all sides. However, before we made this assault on the city, the bishops and priests persuaded all, by exhorting and preaching, to honor the Lord by marching around Jerusalem in a great procession, and to prepare for battle by prayer, fasting, and almsgiving. Early on the sixth day of the week we again attacked the city on all sides, but as the assault was unsuccessful, we were all astounded and fearful. However, when the hour approached on which our Lord Jesus Christ deigned to suffer on the Cross for us, our knights began to fight bravely in one of the towers - namely, the party with Duke Godfrey and his brother, Count Eustace. One of our knights, named Lethold, clambered up the wall of the city, and no sooner had he ascended than the defenders fled from the walls and through the city."

What followed is controversial and unclear, but all of the sources agree that there was a general massacre and that at the very least most of the remaining inhabitants were slaughtered, with many of the inhabitants seeking shelter on the Temple Mount and being cut down by the Crusaders there. According to the *Gesta*:

> "One of our knights, named Lethold, clambered up the wall of the city, and no sooner had he ascended than the defenders fled from the walls and through the city. Our men followed, killing and slaying even to the Temple of Solomon, where the slaughter was so great that our men waded in blood up to their ankles...

> "Count Raymond brought his army and his tower up near the wall from the south, but between the tower and the wall there was a very deep ditch. Then our men took counsel how they might fill it, and had it proclaimed by heralds that anyone who carried three stones to the ditch would receive one denarius. The work of filling it required three days and three nights, and when at length the ditch was filled, they moved the tower up to the wall, but the men defending this portion of the wall fought desperately with stones and fire. When the Count heard that the Franks were already in the city, he said to his men, 'Why do you loiter? Lo, the Franks are even now within the city.' The Emir who commanded the Tower of St. David surrendered to the Count and opened that gate at which the pilgrims had always been accustomed to pay tribute. But this time the pilgrims entered the city, pursuing and killing the Saracens up to the Temple of Solomon, where the enemy gathered in force. The battle raged throughout the day, so that the Temple was covered with their blood. When the pagans had been overcome, our men seized great numbers, both men and women, either killing them or keeping them captive, as they wished. On the roof of the Temple a great number of pagans of both sexes had assembled, and these were taken under the protection of Tancred and Gaston of Beert. Afterward, the army scattered throughout the city and took possession of the gold and silver, the horses and mules, and the houses filled with goods of all kinds."

This account is clearly exaggerated. Aside from the impossibility of riding through a lake of blood, the account is strongly influenced by the Book of Revelation and other apocalyptic books of the Bible. Historians John and Laurita Hill have tied this to Revelation 14:20: "They were trampled in the winepress outside the city, and blood flowed out of the press, rising as high as the horses' bridles for a distance of 1,600 stadia." At the same time, many of the details relate to known tactics of the day.

J. Arthur McFall, author of *Taking Jerusalem: The Climax of the First Crusade*, described it as such: "The Crusaders spent at least that night and the next day killing Muslims, including all of those in the al-Aqsa Mosque, where Tancred's banner should have protected them. Not even women and children were spared. The city's Jews sought refuge in their synagogue, only to be burned alive within it by the Crusaders. Raymond of Aguilers reported that he saw "piles of heads, hands and feet" on a walk through the holy city. Men trotted across the bodies and body fragments as if they were a carpet for their convenience. The Europeans also destroyed the monuments to Orthodox Christian saints and the tomb of Abraham. ... While the slaughter was still going on, many churchmen and princes assembled for a holy procession. Barefoot, chanting and singing, they walked to the shrine of the Holy Sepulchre through the blood flowing around their feet."

Fulcher of Chartres wrote, "At the noon hour on Friday, with trumpets sounding, amid great commotion and shouting "God help us," the Franks entered the city. When the pagans saw one standard planted on the wall, they were completely demoralized, and all their former boldness vanished, and they turned to flee through the narrow streets of the city. Those who were already in rapid flight began to flee more rapidly. Count Raymond and his men, who were attacking the wall on the other side, did not yet know of all this, until they saw the Saracens leap from the wall in front of them. Forthwith, they joyfully rushed into the city to pursue and kill the nefarious enemies, as their comrades were already doing. Some Saracens, Arabs, and Ethiopians took refuge in the tower of David, others fled to the temples of the Lord and of Solomon. A great fight took place in the court and porch of the temples, where they were unable to escape from our gladiators. Many fled to the roof of the temple of Solomon, and were shot with arrows, so that they fell to the ground dead. In this temple almost ten thousand were killed. Indeed, if you had been there you would have seen our feet colored to our ankles with the blood of the slain. But what more shall I relate? None of them were left alive; neither women nor children were spared."

Either way, the assault on the defenders and inhabitants of the city did not end once the city was taken. After a lull overnight, some Crusaders made a sneak attack on those under Tancred's protection on the Temple Mount, where many had sought refuge presumably because it was one of the highest points in the city and sacred to all three major religions. The *Gesta* asserted, "Rejoicing and weeping for joy, our people came to the Sepulchre of Jesus our Saviour to worship and pay their debt [i.e. fulfill crusading vows by worshiping at the Sepulchre]. At dawn our men cautiously went up to the roof of the Temple and attacked Saracen men and women, beheading them with naked swords. Some of the Saracens, however, leaped from the Temple roof. Tancred, seeing this, was greatly angered."

Raymond of Aguilers described it similarly:

"When the city was practically captured by the Franks, the Saracens were still fighting on the other side, where the Count was attacking the wall as though the city should never be captured. But now that our men had possession of the walls and towers, wonderful sights were to be seen. Some of our men (and this was more merciful) cut off the heads of their enemies; others shot them with arrows, so that they fell from the towers; others tortured them longer by casting them into the flames. Piles of heads, hands, and feet were to be seen in the streets of the city. It was necessary to pick one's way over the bodies of men and horses. But these were small matters compared to what happened at the Temple of Solomon, a place where religious services are ordinarily chanted. What happened there? If I tell the truth, it will exceed your powers of belief. So let it suffice to say this much, at least, that in the Temple and porch of Solomon, men rode in blood up to their knees and bridle reins. Indeed, it was a just and splendid judgment of God that this place should be filled with the blood of the unbelievers, since it had suffered so long from their blasphemies. The city was filled with corpses and blood. Some of the enemy took refuge in the Tower of David, and, petitioning Count Raymond for protection, surrendered the Tower into his hands.

Now that the city was taken, it was well worth all our previous labors and hardships to see the devotion of the pilgrims at the Holy Sepulchre. How they rejoiced and exulted and sang a new song to the Lord! For their hearts offered prayers of praise to God, victorious and triumphant, which cannot be told in words. A new day, new joy, new and perpetual gladness, the consummation of our labor and devotion, drew forth from all new words and new songs. This day, I say, will be famous in all future ages, for it turned our labors and sorrows into joy and exultation; this day, I say, marks the justification of all Christianity, the humiliation of paganism, and the renewal of our faith."

A medieval illustration depicting the Church of the Holy Sepulchre

Ibn Qalanisi claimed that all of the Jews were burned alive in their synagogue by chanting Crusaders after taking refuge there, but letters from the contemporary Jewish archive of the Cairo Geniza indicate that some of the Jewish inhabitants survived, most of them having sought refuge with Al-Dawla. According to Raymond of Aguilers and Ibn-al-Athir, Al-Dawla and his men, along with some of the city's inhabitants (including some Jews, according to the letter from the Cairo Geniza), took refuge in the Tower of David. Days later, after a negotiated surrender, they were allowed to leave in the night for Ascalon. Al-Dawla subsequently became governor of Ascalon.

None of the contemporary sources indicate that any Eastern Christians were massacred, which makes sense since they had already been expelled from the city. The *Gesta Francorum* states that Eastern Christian clergy were invited back on August 9, and Fulcher of Chartres reports being greeted by them when he entered the city with Baldwin in 1100. However, this tolerance of Eastern Christians only extended so far; a Latin patriarch (not a Greek one), Arnulf of Chocques, was elected on August 1.

In the wake of the First Crusade, the Dome of the Rock and the al-Aqsa Mosque were transformed into churches (called the Templum Domini–or Temple of God–and Templum Salomonis–or Temple of Solomon–respectively) once all references to Islam had been removed.[49] This included the disposal of prayer rugs, the covering of Arabic calligraphy, and walling up the *mihrab*, or the prayer niche containing the *Qibla* (or direction of prayer), with bricks. When it came to the Dome of the Rock in particular, the Crusaders saw the building as the Templum Domini of the Knights Templar and considered it "to be the veritable Temple of the Lord."[50]

In addition to its change of name and other alterations, one of the most notable modifications made was to cover the rock (the Foundation Stone) with marble. Le Strange quotes from *The Chronicle of Ibn al-Athir for the Crusading Period from al-Kamil fi'l Ta'rikh* to explain this change: "Now the Franks had covered the Rock with a marble pavement...And the reason whereby they had thus covered it with a pavement was this: In the earlier times their priests had been used to (break off and) sell pieces of the Rock to the Frank (pilgrims) who came from beyond the sea on pilgrimage; for these would buy the same for its weight in gold, believing that there lay therein a blessing. But seeing this, certain of the (Latin) kings, fearing les the Rock should all disappear, ordered that it should be paved over to keep it safe."[51]

Any non-Christians left after the Crusader invasion were effectively barred from the area,[52] with some reports indicating that both Jews and Muslims had been expelled from the city altogether. However, there were some very limited incidents of Muslim diplomats being permitted to pray at the site.

Salah ad-Din–often referred to as Saladin in the West–was a Sunni Muslim of Kurdish origin and the founder of the Ayyubid Dynasty, and he took control of Jerusalem in 1187. His capture of Jerusalem was achieved by uniting the feuding Muslim areas that surrounded Jerusalem and using these united forces to push out the Crusaders. Following the First Crusade, most Europeans had returned home, and the forces left in the city were inadequate to prevent the Ayyubid invasion. Despite the mass killings preceding Catholic control of the city, Saladin reportedly refused to respond in kind, barring the massacre of civilians and soldiers and instead ordering them removed from the city.

---

[49] Loewenberg, "Did Jews Abandon the Temple Mount", p. 43.
[50] Le Strange, Palestine under the Moslems, pp. 130.
[51] Le Strange, Palestine under the Moslems, p. 134.
[52] Loewenberg, "Did Jews Abandon the Temple Mount", p. 43.

The Dome of the Rock, the al-Aqsa Mosque, and the location on which they stood was transformed back into a place for Muslim worship[53] and restored "to its pristine condition." The marble covering over the Foundation Stone was removed,[54] along with the furniture and other Christian symbols, and the calligraphy and *mihrab,* which had been covered, was restored. Muslims were permitted to resume prayer at both the Dome of the Rock and the al-Aqsa Mosque, and Jews were reportedly allowed to return to the city. As many Jewish families from North Africa had returned to Jerusalem, many believed their return would lead to the Jewish Redemption promised in the Hebrew Bible.[55] At the same time, Muslim and Christian battles for control of Jerusalem made many Jews fear they were even further away from the Jewish state controlled by Jewish law that many had desired.

After the death of Saladin, his heirs were in conflict and divided up the territories amongst themselves. In the year 1217, Saladin's brother, al-Adil, ordered the destruction of the city's walls as he believed the European Crusaders—now stationed in Acre—stood a good chance of recapturing Jerusalem.[56] In 1229, al-Kamil (Saladin's nephew) negotiated the Treaty of Jaffa. "The Crusaders controlled all of Jerusalem, except for the Temple Mount/Haram al-Sharif, which remained in Moslem hands with the proviso the Crusaders be permitted to visit the site."[57] While this did prevent another massive bloodshed, al-Kamil was regarded as a traitor by many Muslims in the region for negotiating with the European invaders.

Over the next few hundred years, Jerusalem was again attacked by disparate Muslim groups, European Crusaders, the Tatars, and the Mongols. The Ayyubids allied initially with the Central Asian Tatars with the hope they would drive the Crusaders out. When they attacked Jerusalem, they killed as many as 6,000 Crusaders and destroyed churches and homes.[58] Later, following negotiations between the Mamluk class of Egypt and another Ayyubid rival ruler, the Mamluks took control of Jerusalem in 1250. The city served more as tax revenue for their capital at Cairo. "Despite the incompetence of their rule, the Mamluks built well all the cities of their realm, and nowhere more beautifully than in Jerusalem."[59] The Mamluks rebuilt the city and Muslim immigrants from around the region flocked Jerusalem, thus changing the religious face of the city back to being predominantly Muslim once again.

The Ottoman Empire

In 1516, the Muslim Ottoman Empire took over Jerusalem. The Egyptian Mamluks fell easily to the Ottoman firepower acquired in allegiances with European and Asian rulers. It was Sultan Suleiman the Magnificent who oversaw reconstruction of the walls surrounding Jerusalem.

[53] Ibid, p. 44.
[54] Le Strange, Palestine under the Moslems, pp. 133-4.
[55] Karen Armstrong, *Jerusalem*, p. 299.
[56] Eric H. Cline, *Jerusalem Besieged*, p. 204.
[57] Ibid, p. 206.
[58] Ibid, p. 213.
[59] Thomas A. Idinopulos, Jerusalem Blessed, Jerusalem Cursed, p. 259.

Although Jews had been barred from ascending to the area housing the Dome of the Rock and the al-Aqsa Mosque, he did permit—and even guarantee—the right of Jews to pray at the Western Wall, a remnant of the destroyed Second Temple.[60] This came after Jewish law had largely agreed that it was impermissible for Jews to visit there anyway, due to concern they might inadvertently walk over a location to which, in the time of the Temple, was forbidden except to high priests. In Jewish tradition, during the days of the Temple, it was only permitted for priests of the tribe of Levi (one of the 12 sons of Jacob) to enter certain areas of the Temple Mount. Until the Temple was restored, many Jews felt believed these areas forbidden.

Suleiman the Magnificent

While the Ottomans appeared to show some concern for the religious diversity of the Holy City, some reports claim the Ottoman Empire "invested little effort in the upkeep of the Dome of the Rock or al-Aqsa Mosque."[61] It is likely that as the Ottomans spread their control in the

[60] Loewenberg, "Did Jews Abandon the Temple Mount", p. 45.
[61] Loewenberg, "Did Jews Abandon the Temple Mount", p. 45.

Levant, Mesopotamia, and North Africa, their concern for particular upkeep proved difficult as the empire had overextended itself. Besides, according to Thomas Idinopulos, the Ottomans considered themselves more the heirs of the Persian Empire's cultural and linguistic heritage than that of the Arab Muslims. "The sultan deliberately excluded them from civil administration, and virtually all the military, legal, and civil business of the empire was run by the Janissaries, the grownup children of Christian slaves converted to Islam and especially trained to serve only the sultan."[62]

As the empire stopped expanding—having bucked up against the edge of European Christian empires as those encroached in India, Africa, and North America—the Ottoman Empire made its infamous decline. Agricultural production weakened, trade was in crisis, and the taxes increased among the dhimmi population of Jews and Christians in the empire. A succession of Ottoman sultans attempted to implement reforms on the empire, putting the Ottomans in a position to rival their growing European counterparts, but their disregard for Jerusalem in their overall control of the empire left the Holy City open to increasing control and influence by Jewish and Christian allies in Europe.

During the reign of Muhammad Ali—an Albanian Mamluk who rose through the ranks to take control of Egypt and much of the Ottoman Empire during the 19th century—Europeans made their way to Jerusalem at Ali's request.[63] Muhammad Ali had hoped to gain the support of Western powers against the remainder of the Ottoman Empire and his Arab rivals in the Arabian Peninsula. "Thus for the first time a Western power was able to establish a consulate in Jerusalem—a step which the local people had fought for so long."[64]

[62] Thomas A. Idinopulos, Jerusalem Blessed, Jerusalem Cursed, p. 265.
[63] Karen Armstrong, *Jerusalem*, p. 351.
[64] Ibid, p. 351.

Muhammad Ali

As European emissaries made their way into the Holy Land and beyond, European influence found strong support among existing Jews and Christians. William Young—a British diplomat—was told to support the cause of European Jews in the Holy Land, no doubt part of the Christian desire to lead Jews back to Jerusalem with the hope of ushering in the Second Coming of Jesus Christ. The Jewish population of Jerusalem increased once more, and European powers worked to intensify the Christian influence in the city, as well.

The Ottomans were able to work with the British, French, and Russians to force Muhammad Ali's dynasty out of Jerusalem in 1840, which helped them fully solidify European foundations for control that would take full effect after World War I. Just as in other areas of colonial control,

European states found different ways to divide, conquer, and develop advantageous relationships with local leaders that would benefit them on down the line. The alliance of the Ottoman Empire with these European powers was, no doubt, the final nail in the coffin of the "sick man of Europe," foreshadowing the end of one of history's longest—and definitely the longest reigning Muslim—empires the world had ever seen.

The British Mandate

In the waning days of the Ottoman Empire, the lands of the Middle East and North Africa were fraught with rebellion and violence. New and foreign ideas surged as people from Europe and the Middle East traveled between regions sharing thoughts on the future of mankind. Ideas about nationalism and patriotism meshed well with the new desire for Arab independence from foreign influence, particularly from their Ottoman rulers. "Nationalism emerged in the Arab provinces of the Ottoman Empire at the start of the twentieth century. It was at first difficult for the Arab peoples of the empire to imagine themselves in a separate state after nearly four centuries under Ottoman rule."[65] Nationalists came in all flavors, favoring democracies, autocracies, theocracies. The Ottomans felt they were all threats and those who believed such ideas were exiled to Europe. While there, the exiles further refined their ideas, affected by the Enlightenment philosophies and literature flourishing in Europe at the time.

The Ottomans' final mistake was their alliance with Germany in 1914. In the past, the Ottomans had worked with any European power able to quell internal unrest and hopefully boost their failing economy, but they quickly saw the undesirable effects of British and French influence in the empire, particularly in Syria, Palestine, and Iraq. Caught up in the Entente between the British, French, and Russians, the Ottomans fell, along with their German allies, at the end of the World War I.

Following World War I, the newly formed League of Nations–the precursor to the United Nations–established the Mandate System in order to administer territory previously under the Ottoman Empire. This included the area covering modern-day Israel and the Palestinian territories, which were placed under British control and collectively named Palestine. The territory east of the Jordan River was carved out of the Mandate of Palestine and became Transjordan (modern-day Jordan), which was also British-controlled but under the rule of the Sharif of Mecca's son. This family's claim to leadership was derived from their status as Hashemites, a clan that claims to descend from the Prophet Muhammad.

The idea of the Mandate System, stipulated under Article 22 of The Covenant of the League of Nations, was to resolve the situation of territory that was, after World War I, no longer under the control of their prior ruler but "inhabited by peoples not yet able to stand by themselves under the strenuous conditions of the modern world." Each mandate had to "differ according to the

---

[65] Eugen Rogan, *The Arabs: A History*, p. 182.

state of the development of the people, the geographical situation of the territory, its economic conditions and other similar circumstances," and the ruling entity required to submit "an annual report in reference to the territory committed to its charge."[66] In short, the goal of the mandate system was to ensure the development of the territory under their control with the ultimate aim of independence, but the ways in which this was implemented had to be in-line with the growing procedures and norms developed by the state system of Western powers. Borders were important, as was sovereignty, but keeping the colonial lands of the Mandates at an arm's length was important, since European control was not seen as benevolent, but rather, as a necessity to ensure the further development of the British and French empires. In practice, independence was not achieved until after World War II and the advent of the League of Nation's successor, due to violent revolutions in all previous colonial territories in the Middle East, Asia, and Africa.

Since the 1880s, throngs of Jewish immigrants from Europe and Russia have fled to Jerusalem and the surrounding lands. In 1917, the World Zionist Congress convened a conference, and after years of lobbying for the British government's support of Jewish ownership of the Palestinian territories—in particular Jerusalem—Jewish Zionist leaders gained the support of Prime Minister David Lloyd George and Foreign Minister Arthur Balfour. In a letter dated November 2, 1917, Balfour reported to [Zionist leader Chaim] Weizmann, "His Majesty's Government view with favour [sic] the establishment in Palestine of a national home for the Jewish people, and will use their best endeavors to facilitate the achievement of this object, it being clearly understood that nothing shall be down which may prejudice the civil and religious rights of existing non-Jewish communities in Palestine, or the rights and political status enjoyed by Jews in any other country."[67]

---

[66] "The Covenant of the League of Nations" Article 22, December 1924, available at http://avalon.law.yale.edu/20th_century/leagcov.asp.
[67] Eugene Rogan, *The Arabs: A History*, p. 191.

Balfour

The British saw the Balfour Declaration as a political move, knowing that most of the incoming Jewish populations were American and Russian, which would help them win the favor of these communities. Also, with allies in Palestine, the British would be able to secure control over the Suez Canal, something they did not feel they could count on with Muslim control of the Arabian Peninsula and Egypt.

As the Jewish population of Jerusalem and surrounding cities increased, skirmishes between Jews, Arab Muslims, and Christians significantly increased. The Arab Higher Committee was created in 1936 and called for strikes and revolts by Arab workers in Palestine, which led to an increase of 20,000 British troops in Palestine.[68] When the Arab kings of the region—who had gained legitimacy and power only through their recent alliances with the British—called on their

---

[68] Ibid, p. 254.

Palestinian Arab neighbors to end their revolts, the tides of Arab unity shifted. It was at this point the division of Arab Muslim and Christian interests may be found; while nationalism was still very much a prevalent force among inhabitants of the Middle East, territorial sovereignty and the establishment of global norms through the rising state system developed by European powers prevented much action on the part of the Arab states. Over the next several decades, there was a resumption of wars between Arab leaders against Israel, but the feeling of unification of Arab Muslims is used more as a rallying cry among Arab leaders like Egyptian President Gamal Abd el Nasser than something that might actually be realized at the end of the wars.

As Europe once more edged toward war, European preoccupation with colonial politics took a back seat, and as violence continued in Palestine, the British looked to put down resistance and terrorism perpetuated by Jewish groups. In 1939, the British issued a White Paper, which limited Jewish immigration to 75,000 over the next five years, leading to further Jewish violence, this time against British colonialists in Jerusalem.[69] A series of terrorist attacks by the Irgun—a Jewish paramilitary organization—against the British culminated in 1946 with the bombing of the King David Hotel in downtown Jerusalem.

Following the conclusion of World War II, in 1947 the British government announced its intention to revert the mandate to the United Nations. Later that year, committees were established to propose a solution to the situation in Mandatory Palestine, referring to competing interests in the territory. After the revelations of fascist Germany's concentration camps and "Final Solution" plan, which sought to exterminate the Jewish population and resulted in the deaths of some six million Jews, pressure had increased upon Britain to allow for increased Jewish immigration for wartime survivors. Arab leaders, however, opposed the establishment of a Jewish state in Palestine. For example, the king of Saudi Arabia at the time, King Abdulaziz ibn Abdul Rahman Al Saud, told President Franklin D. Roosevelt in their famous meeting in February 1945 aboard the USS *Quincy* on Great Bitter Lake that the crimes of fascist Germany did not justify Jewish immigration to Arab lands. He told Roosevelt to "give them and their descendants the choicest lands and homes of the Germans who had oppressed them."[70]

The Partition Plan carved up two strange looking states, but their motive was to create an Israel in which the Jewish population was a 55% majority, while Palestine had an over 90% Palestinian Arab majority. Meanwhile, the city of Jerusalem would be administered internationally, due to the sensitive religious concerns of Muslims, Christians, and Jews. In addition to several Christian holy spots, Jerusalem's Al-Aqsa Mosque is the third holiest site in Islam, and it is situated right next to the Western Wall, the Jews' holiest remaining site.

---

[69] Eric H. Cline, *Jerusalem Besieged*, p. 255.
[70] William A. Eddy, *F.D.R. Meets Ibn Saud* (Washington, D.C., America-Mideast Educational & Training Services, Inc., 1954), p. 32.

The proposed plan was accepted by the Jewish Agency, which represented the leaders of the Jewish community in Palestine. However, it was rejected by Palestinian leaders in the Mandate, and it was also rejected by the newly formed Arab League, a confederation of Middle Eastern Arab states led by Egypt, Lebanon, Iraq, Saudi Arabia, Syria, and Yemen. Although the partitioned state of Israel would have had a Jewish majority, the remainder of the British Mandate after the partition of Jordan was about 2/3 Palestinian, and they viewed the plan as being unfairly advantageous to the Jews.

The British were still in control of the Mandate, and they accepted the U.N. Partition Plan, but they had no interest in attempting to enforce the partition of the two states, especially not over the objections of one side after British forces had already been subjected to violence by Jewish groups. And without the British, there was no way for the United Nations to enforce the partition.

Therefore, in September 1947, the British announced that they would be wiping their hands clean of the entire Mandate on May 14, 1948. On May 14, 1948, the British Mandate officially expired. That same day, the Jewish National Council issued the Declaration of the Establishment of the State of Israel. About 10 minutes later, President Truman officially recognized the State of Israel, and the Soviet Union also quickly recognized Israel.

However, the Palestinians and the Arab League did not recognize the new state, and the very next day, armies from Egypt, Syria, Lebanon and Iraq invaded the former British Mandate to squelch Israel, while Saudi Arabia assisted the Arab armies. Jordan would also get involved in the war, fighting the Israelis around Jerusalem. Initially, the Arab armies numbered over 20,000 soldiers, but the Zionist militia groups like the Lehi, Irgun and Haganah made it possible for Israel to quickly assemble the Israel Defense Forces, still known today simply as the IDF. By the end of 1948, the Israelis had over 60,000 soldiers and the Arab armies numbered over 50,000.

The Israelis began pressing their advantages on both land and air by the fall of 1948, bombing foreign capitals like Damascus while overrunning Arab armies in the British Mandate. In towns like Ramat Rachel and Deir Yassin, close quarter combat in villages led to civilian casualties and charges of massacres. In particular, the Jewish assault on Deir Yassin, which led to the death of about 50 Palestinians, is often labeled a massacre by the Palestinians, although the Israelis asserted that house to house combat made fighting difficult.

Regardless, Palestinians who heard of the news of Jewish attacks on places like Deir Yassin were afraid for their lives and began to flee their homes. At the same time, Palestinians were encouraged by commanders of the Arab armies to clear out of the area until after they could defeat Israel. Palestinians and Jews had been fighting since 1947, and over 250,000 Palestinians had already fled their homes by the time the 1948 War had started. It is unclear how many Palestinians fled from Jewish forces and how many left voluntarily, but by the end of the war over 700,000 Palestinians had fled from their homes in the former British Mandate. Meanwhile, nearly 800,000 Jews had been forcibly expelled from their homes in nations throughout the Middle East, leading to an influx of Jews at the same time Palestinians were leaving.

In late 1948, Israel was on the offensive. That December, the U.N. General Assembly passed Resolution 194, which declared that under a peace agreement, "refugees wishing to return to their homes and live in peace with their neighbors should be permitted to do so," and "compensation should be paid for the property of those choosing not to return." Months later, Israel began signing armistices with Egypt, Jordan, and Syria, which left Israel in control of nearly 75% of the lands that were to be partitioned into the two states under the 1947 plan. Jordan now occupied Judea and Samaria, which later became known as the West Bank due to its position on the western bank of the Jordan River. Jordan also occupied three quarters of Jerusalem, with the Israelis controlling only about a quarter in the western part of the city. To the west, Egypt occupied the Gaza Strip. The Palestinians and their supporters often argue that Palestinian refugees have the right to return to their land under General Assembly Resolution 194. The Israelis and their supporters assert that Resolution 194 requires a peace agreement and that the refugees who are to return must wish to live in peace.

The new armistice lines became known as the "Green Line," a common term still used today.

Jordanian Control of Jerusalem

Jordan maintained control over Jerusalem's Old City and the West Bank until the 1967 war, also known as the Six Day War. After taking control over the territory during the 1948 conflict and following the 1950 Parliamentary elections in which Palestinians were granted representation, the West Bank and East Jerusalem were formally annexed. The annexation was "widely regarded as illegal and void," including by the Arab League. In fact, only Britain, Iraq, and Pakistan recognized the move.[71] The country was, at that time, ruled by King Abdullah, the son of Sharif Hussein of Mecca. The annexation was reportedly done in opposition to the former Mufti of Jerusalem, who wanted to see the creation of an Arab state in Palestine under his own leadership.

Jordan also took a step that no other Arab states offered to Palestinian refugees by offering full Jordanian citizenship. Not long after, King Abdullah I, the ruler at the time, was assassinated in Jerusalem at the entrance to the al-Aqsa Mosque on July 20, 1951. King Abdullah's bodyguards subsequently fatally shot his assassin, identified as a Palestinian Arab named Mustafa Shukri Ashshu. Ashshu was a 21-year-old tailor living in the Old City who had fought during the 1948 conflict with forces associated with the former Mufti of Jerusalem, described as "a bitter political

---

[71] Eyal Benvenisti, *The International Law of Occupation* (New Jersey: Princeton University Press, 1993), p. 108. See also Richard Cavendish, "Jordan Formally Annexes the West Bank", *History Today* Vol. 50, Issue 4 (April 2000).

enemy of King Abdullah."[72] Violence once again flared following the assassination of King Abdullah, and the Arab League quelled the Arab rioters who had protested against the new King Hussein.[73]

Although there were clauses in the armistice agreement stipulating that Jews be granted access to the Old City, Jordan did not, in fact, permit such access. This was based on the argument that Israel's refusal to allow Palestinians to return to their homes in territory under Israel's control voided the clause.[74] In fact, this restriction was so great that "tourists entering East Jerusalem had to present baptismal certificates or other proof they were not Jewish."[75]

Less than 20 years after the 1948 war, Jordanian control of East Jerusalem ended with the Arab-Israeli conflict of 1967. The U.S. Office of the Historian describes this war as "mark[ing] the failure of the Eisenhower, Kennedy, and Johnson administrations' efforts to prevent renewed Arab-Israeli conflict following the 1956 Suez War."[76] The 1967 conflict was preceded by a false report from the then-Soviet Union that Israel was amassing troops along Syria's border, triggering Egypt to deploy its own troops into the Sinai. Egyptian President Gamal Abdul Nasser ordered the United Nations Emergency Force (UNEF), established following the Suez War to monitor the cessation of hostilities,[77] to withdraw in May. Once this had been done, Nasser announced, on May 22, that he would close the Straits of Tiran,[78] which Israel considered to be an act of war. In a 1957 statement to the UNGA, Israel's foreign minister stated that "[i]nterference, by armed force, with ships of Israeli flag exercising free and innocent passage in the Gulf of Aqaba and through the Straits of Tiran will be regarded by Israel as an attack entitling it to exercise its inherent right of self-defence under Article 51 of the Charter and to take all such measures as are necessary to ensure the free and innocent passage of its ships in the Gulf and in the straits."[79]

---

[72] "Assassination of King Abdullah", *The Guardian*, 21 July 1951.

[73] Eric H. Cline, *Jerusalem Besieged*, p 284.

[74] Michael Dumper, Jerusalem Unbound: Geography, History, and the Future of the Holy City (New York: Columbia University Press, 2014), p. 48.

[75] Roger Friedland and Richard Hecht, *To Rule Jerusalem* (Berkeley: University of California Press, 2000), p. 39.

[76] "The 1967 Aarb-Israeli War", *US Office of the Historian*.

[77] United Nations Emergency Force I, *United Nations Peacekeeping Missions*, http://www.un.org/en/peacekeeping/missions/past/unef1backgr2.html.

[78] The 1967 Aarb-Israeli War", *US Office of the Historian*.

[79] "Statement to the General Assembly by Foreign Minister Meir", *Israel Ministry of Foreign Affairs*, 1 March 1957.

Nasser

Following the closure of the Straits of Tiran, Jordan and Syria "declared their solidarity with Egypt if there was to be a conflict."[80] Concerns regarding war were also demonstrated by Nasser's statement at the end of May to the Egyptian National Assembly, in which he stated that Egypt "would decide the time and place and that we must prepare ourselves in order to win…preparations have already been made. We are now ready to confront Israel."[81] According to the US Embassy, "Nasser genuinely believed that the Arab states were capable of crushing Israel on the battlefield and that every single Egyptian official the embassy had spoken to shared this belief."[82] As a result of these events, as well as a perception that Western powers would not intercede to open the Straits of Tiran, Israel launched a pre-emptive strike on June 5, 1967. Despite Nasser's belief in the strength of the armies of the Arab states, the conflict–as its moniker, the Six Day War, indicates–lasted only six days and ended with an Israeli victory.

The results of the Six Day War created several issues that have still not been resolved in the Middle East. Israel now found itself in possession of territories that were the home of over a million Arabs. Of these territories, Israel officially annexed only East Jerusalem and the Golan

[80] Ariel Colonomos, *The Gamble of War: Is It Possible to Justify Preventive War* (New York: Palgrave MacMillan, 2013), p. 25.
[81] "Nasser's Speech to the Egyptian National Assembly", 29 May 1967 as quoted in Moshe Gat, *Conflict in the Middle East, 1964-1967: The coming of the Six-Day War* (Connecticut: Praeger, 2003), p. 219.
[82] Gat, Conflict in the Middle East, p. 219.

Heights, leaving the inhabitants of the West Bank, Sinai Peninsula, and Gaza Strip in limbo regarding citizenship status.

On November 22, 1967, the United Nations Security Council passed Resolution 242, still one of the central resolutions of the conflict. Creating the "land for peace" formula, the resolution called for "[t]ermination of all claims or states of belligerency and respect for and acknowledgment of the sovereignty, territorial integrity and political independence of every State in the area and their right to live in peace within secure and recognized boundaries free from threats or acts of force."

In exchange for the Arab nations ending their belligerency and acknowledging Israel's sovereignty, Resolution 242 called for the "[w]ithdrawal of Israel armed forces from territories occupied in the recent conflict." This is one of the most important and most misunderstood aspects of the resolution. Although a simple reading of the language seems to call upon Israel to return to the Green Line and give back all of the lands captured during the Six Day War, the U.N. diplomats did not intend for that. The language intentionally left out the word "the" in front of the word territories, an indication that the resolution did not call upon Israel to return to the Green Line before the Six Day War of 1967. Resolution 242 was drafted by the British, whose U.N. Ambassador, Lord Caradon, later said, "It would have been wrong to demand that Israel return to its positions of June 4, 1967, because those positions were undesirable and artificial. After all, they were just the places where the soldiers of each side happened to be on the day the fighting stopped in 1948. They were just armistice lines. That's why we didn't demand that the Israelis return to them." Similarly, the American U.N. Ambassador said, "The notable omissions – which were not accidental – in regard to withdrawal are the words "the" or "all" and the "June 5, 1967 lines" ... the resolution speaks of withdrawal from occupied territories without defining the extent of withdrawal... Israel's prior frontiers had proved to be notably Insecure."

Israeli Control of Jerusalem

Shortly after the conclusion of the 1967 war, East Jerusalem was formally annexed by the Israeli government, and in 1980, the entire city was declared the country's undivided capital. Both declarations faced significant international opposition, and East Jerusalem continues to be considered occupied territory (along with the West Bank and the Golan Heights) by most of the international community. As a result, the vast majority of embassies to Israel are situated in Tel Aviv and not Jerusalem. This is true even for the country's strongest allies.

Since 1967, Israel has permitted all faiths entry to Jerusalem's Old City, and likely as a means of avoiding conflict, it has permitted the Islamic Waqf, established by Jordan when Jerusalem was under its control, to retain authority over the Temple Mount/al-Aqsa Mosque Compound. However, tensions in–and interest over–this location have continued, and not only between Jews and Muslims; some more conservative sects of Christianity, for example, believe the return of

Jesus Christ will not happen until the Jews have gathered in Israel and the Third Jewish Temple in Jerusalem is rebuilt. Thus, in 1969, an Australian man, named Denis Michael Rohan, started a fire at the site, believing the destruction of the al-Aqsa Mosque would allow for construction of the third temple, and as a result, the coming of Jesus. He was later deemed insane.[83]

In the wake of that event, Arab sources have lobbed accusations that the fire had been set by Jews. In a 2002 article in the Saudi Arabian English newspaper, *Arab News*, the event is described as having occurred when "Zionist aggressors set fire to Al-Aqsa." It goes on to claim that "Zionist gangs acted with the support of Israeli occupation forces…[as] part of the ongoing Israeli aggressions against the mosque."[84] This fire, and general concern regarding the al-Aqsa Mosque, were some of the factors leading to the 1969 creation of the Organization of the Islamic Conference, which later became the Organization of Islamic Cooperation (OIC), and which met in Rabat, Morocco, one month after the fire. According to Mohsen M. Saleh, "The arson of *al-Aqsa* and the role of the Muslims in facing such challenges was the heart of discussions" at the Rabat meeting.[85]

Although a Christian man was responsible for the 1969 fire, radical Jews in the 1980s were responsible for a failed plot to blow up the Dome of the Rock. An Israeli messianic group, known as the Gush Emunim (Hebrew for "Block of the Faithful") Underground, was responsible for a number of anti-Arab attacks, such as the placement of explosives in the vehicles of local Palestinian leaders, in response to an attack on Jews in Hebron.[86] In 1984, a number of members were arrested for involvement in these attacks and for planning to blow up the Dome of the Rock. Yehuda Etzion, one of the members who had conceived the plot, told other members that "the removal of the Muslim mosques [on the Temple Mount/al-Aqsa Mosque Compound] would spark a new light in the nation and would trigger a major spiritual revolution in the direction of intense religiosity and commitment to redemption." Their final target was determined to have been the Dome of the Rock.[87]

The First Intifada was a Palestinian uprising that broke out in 1987 against the Israeli occupation, triggering protests in the Gaza Strip, West Bank, and East Jerusalem. The Palestinians mostly protested with strikes, boycotts, and rock throwing, although Hamas and the PLO also engaged in violent attacks, including a suicide bombing, that killed over 150 Israelis.

---

[83] "Madman at the Mosque", *TIME Magazine*, 12 January 1970 and "The Burning of al-Aqsa", *TIME Magazine*, 29 August 1969.

[84] "33rd anniversary of Al-Aqsa Mosque's burning", *Arab News*, 21 August 2002. See also Dov Lieber, "PA, Hamas recycle lie 'radical Jew' set fire to Al-Aqsa Mosque", *The Times of Israel*, 21 August 2016.

[85] Mohsen M. Saleh, "The Arson of *al-Aqsa* Mosque in 1969 and its Impact on the Muslim World As Reflected in the British Documents", *Dirasat* Vol. 33, No. 2 (2006), p. 421.

[86] Ehud Sprinzak, "From Messianic Pioneering to Vigilante Terrorism: The Case of the Gush Emunim Underground", p. 199 in David C. Rapoport (ed.), *Inside Terrorist Organizations* (London: Frank Cass Publishers, 2001) and Motti Inbari, *Jewish Fundamentalism and the Temple Mount: Who Will Build the Third Temple* (New York: State University of New York, 2009), p. 51.

[87] Sprinzak, "From Messianic Pioneering to Vigilante Terrorism", p. 194, 199 and Inbari, *Jewish Fundamentalism*, pp. 55, 68.

Underscoring the animosity between the PLO and the Islamic factions like Hamas and Islamic Jihad, intra-Palestinian violence also killed 1,000 Palestinians who were alleged to be Israeli collaborators. During the First Intifada, Israeli forces also killed over a thousand Palestinians. The First Intifada was never a directly controlled uprising, and no Palestinian leaders expected it to make permanent changes in the ongoing conflict, but it was directly responsible for the Madrid Conference of 1991, which would put in motion all of the pieces that make up today's peace process formulations.

Despite the intense negotiations that took place in 2000 and January 2001, the peace process was ultimately derailed during the Second Intifada. Both sides have long argued over what triggered the Second Intifada. The Palestinian Authority claimed the Second Intifada was a natural, uncoordinated uprising triggered by Likud leader Ariel Sharon's visit to the Temple Mount in September 2000, as well as the inability to reach a satisfactory deal at Camp David the previous July. Palestinians in Jerusalem protesting Sharon's visit began rioting.

The Israelis would later assert that Arafat himself had planned the Second Intifada and that Palestinian leaders waited for the right moment to start the fighting. Fatah official Marwan Barghouti, later imprisoned by Israel for his role in attacks during the Second Intifada, admitted, "After Sharon left, I remained for two hours in the presence of other people, we discussed the manner of response and how it was possible to react in all the cities and not just in Jerusalem." One of Hamas' top leaders, Mahmoud al-Zahar, also claimed that Arafat ordered Hamas and Fatah's militant wing, the al-Aqsa Martyrs Brigade, to begin launching attacks against Israel once he realized Camp David would not be successful.

Since 2000, as a means of reducing tensions, Jews have been barred from praying on the Temple Mount, although they are not restricted from visiting the site. In addition, no non-Muslims are permitted entry into the Dome of the Rock, where the Foundation Stone stands. This is separate from the self-imposed restriction by many religious Jews who will not walk there out of concern they may unknowingly walk in the area where the "Holy of Holies" once stood, referring to the inner sanctum of the historic Jewish Temple that tradition claims once housed the Ark of the Covenant (hence the Jewish reference to the location as the "Temple Mount"). Others argue that Jewish prayer ought to be permitted, given the site's status as the holiest for Jews.

The policy barring Jewish prayer is enforced by Israeli police forces stationed at the Temple Mount/al-Aqsa Mosque Compound. It has not, however, resulted in the complete cessation of tensions. Rather, the al-Aqsa Mosque–particularly claims that Israel is attempting to take over the site–remains a rallying call for those opposed to Israeli occupation, or the existence of Israel in general (such as Hamas, the group that currently governs the Gaza Strip, which states its complete opposition to a Jewish state in its Charter).

In 2016, for example, the "knife intifada," which referred to a wave of Palestinian nationals stabbing Israelis, broke out amid allegations spreading across Palestinian society that Israel was attempting to establish a permanent Jewish presence at the Temple Mount/al-Aqsa Mosque Compound. The other parts are related to age and gender limitations sometimes placed on Muslim entry into Israel during times of existing or expected tension (usually limiting younger male entry), and the extreme sensitivity of the location to Muslims.

The Palestinian Liberation Organization (PLO), the precursor to the Palestinian Authority (PA), declared Jerusalem as the capital of the State of Palestine in the 1988 Palestinian Declaration of Independence, proclaimed by then-leader Yasser Arafat. He stated, "The Palestine National Council announces in the name of God, in the name of the people, of the Arab Palestinian people, the establishment of the state of Palestine in our Palestinian nation, with holy Jerusalem as its capital."[88] In 2002, Arafat formally signed into a law a bill naming Jerusalem as the Palestinian capital, seen as a response to a proposed U.S. law officially recognizing the city as Israel's capital.[89]

Ehud Barak, Bill Clinton, and Yasser Arafat

The fact that two parties consider Jerusalem as their capital is so diplomatically contentious that it is considered a final status issue for the ongoing peace process, meaning it's expected to be tackled last. This is in contrast to the issue of borders, regarding which both parties have nominally agreed will be determined by the Green Line with land swaps permitting the largest

---

[88] Youssef M. Ibrahim, "P.L.O Proclaims Palestine to be an Independent State, Hints at Recognizing Israel", *The New York Times*, 15 November 1988.
[89] Arafat names Jerusalem as capital", *BBC News*, 6 October 2002.

Israeli settlements in the West Bank to become a part of the Jewish state. In 2014, Israel's Knesset (Parliament) passed a law requiring any division of Jerusalem be determined by national referendum. In response, Israeli parties opposed to the bill described it as an attempt to preemptively destroy the potential for a peace agreement.[90]

Recently, there has been a renewed call for moving the U.S. Embassy to Jerusalem. This call has come from President Donald Trump and was a cornerstone of his foreign policy speeches during his campaign for presidency in 2016. These calls were bolstered by evangelical Protestant Christians in the U.S. who are traditionally conservative and Republican. The position is also supported by a large swathe of the American Jewish community.

While Trump's presidency is still very much in its early stages, the new administration has already had various discussions with Israeli Prime Minister Benjamin Netanyahu and seems to have come to some agreement that the U.S. Embassy may eventually move to Jerusalem. Indeed, such a proclamation has already riled Muslim communities around the world, and others view it as going against the longstanding American tradition of avoiding getting in the middle of the conflict and taking sides, despite staunch support for Israel's right to defend its borders and people. Now that the American administration has brought the issue to the forefront, once again, the world waits to see what steps will be taken and when.

As all of this history makes clear, Jerusalem—the Holy City for the world's largest religions— remains an important site for 1.5 billion Muslims around the globe. Its significance for Jews and Christians helped to establish its initial importance in the eyes of the early Muslims, but it was reinforced during the reign of several Muslim rulers over nearly 1,500 years. Jerusalem houses the al-Aqsa Mosque and the Dome of the Rock, the two most important religious sites for Muslims outside of Mecca and Medina, and Muslims believe these locations were important in the life of the Prophet Muhammad and his nascent religious following during the 7th and 8th centuries. The fact that so many invaders—both Muslim and non-Muslim alike—have decided it was important to control Jerusalem serves to entrench deep feelings of ownership and control among Muslims.

The current political realities of Jerusalem and Israel, in general, make finding a solution for the conflict even more difficult. Those who study the conflict and history generally focus on its intractable nature, particularly when they look to the city's past, which is fraught with violence and invasion.

Online Resources

Other books about Islamic history by Charles River Editors

Other books about Jerusalem on Amazon

---

[90] Aaron Magid, "As the Israeli people if they want peace", *Haaretz*, 19 March 2014.

Bibliography

Ahmed, Akbar (1999). Islam Today: A Short Introduction to the Muslim World (2.00 ed.). I. B. Tauris. ISBN 978-1-86064-257-9.

Bennett, Clinton (2010). Interpreting the Qur'an: a guide for the uninitiated. Continuum International Publishing Group. p. 101. ISBN 978-0-8264-9944-8.

Brockopp, Jonathan E. (2003). Islamic Ethics of Life: abortion, war and euthanasia. University of South Carolina press. ISBN 1-57003-471-0.

Esposito, John (2010). Islam: The Straight Path (4th ed.). Oxford University Press. ISBN 978-0-19-539600-3.

Esposito, John (2000b). Oxford History of Islam. Oxford University Press. ISBN 978-0-19-510799-9.

Esposito, John (2002a). Unholy War: Terror in the Name of Islam. Oxford University Press. ISBN 978-0-19-516886-0.

Esposito, John (2002b). What Everyone Needs to Know about Islam. Oxford University Press. ISBN 0-19-515713-3.

Farah, Caesar (2003). Islam: Beliefs and Observances (7th ed.). Barron's Educational Series. ISBN 978-0-7641-2226-2.

Firestone, Reuven (1999). Jihad: The Origin of Holy War in Islam. Oxford University Press. ISBN 0-19-512580-0.

Goldschmidt, Jr., Arthur; Lawrence Davidson (2005). A Concise History of the Middle East (8th ed.). Westview Press. ISBN 978-0-8133-4275-7.

Hawting, G. R. (2000). The First Dynasty of Islam: The Umayyad Caliphate AD 661–750. Routledge. ISBN 0-415-24073-5.

Hedayetullah, Muhammad (2006). Dynamics of Islam: An Exposition. Trafford Publishing. ISBN 978-1-55369-842-5.

Hofmann, Murad (2007). Islam and Qur'an. ISBN 978-1-59008-047-4.

Hourani, Albert; Ruthven, Malise (2003). A History of the Arab Peoples. Belknap Press; Revised edition. ISBN 978-0-674-01017-8.

Kramer, Martin (1987). Shi'ism, Resistance, and Revolution. Westview Press. ISBN 978-0-

8133-0453-3.

Lapidus, Ira (2002). A History of Islamic Societies (2nd ed.). Cambridge University Press. ISBN 978-0-521-77933-3.

Lewis, Bernard (1984). The Jews of Islam. Routledge & Kegan Paul. ISBN 0-7102-0462-0.

Lewis, Bernard (1993). The Arabs in History. Oxford University Press. ISBN 0-19-285258-2.

Lewis, Bernard (1997). The Middle East. Scribner. ISBN 978-0-684-83280-7.

Lewis, Bernard (2001). Islam in History: Ideas, People, and Events in the Middle East (2nd ed.). Open Court. ISBN 978-0-8126-9518-2.

Lewis, Bernard (2003). What Went Wrong?: The Clash Between Islam and Modernity in the Middle East (Reprint ed.). Harper Perennial. ISBN 978-0-06-051605-5.

Lewis, Bernard (2004). The Crisis of Islam: Holy War and Unholy Terror. Random House, Inc., New York. ISBN 978-0-8129-6785-2.

Madelung, Wilferd (1996). The Succession to Muhammad: A Study of the Early Caliphate. Cambridge University Press. ISBN 0-521-64696-0.

Momen, Moojan (1987). An Introduction to Shi`i Islam: The History and Doctrines of Twelver Shi`ism. Yale University Press. ISBN 978-0-300-03531-5.

Nigosian, Solomon Alexander (2004). Islam: its history, teaching, and practices. Indiana University Press.

Peters, F. E. (2003). Islam: A Guide for Jews and Christians. Princeton University Press. ISBN 0-691-11553-2.

Rippin, Andrew (2001). Muslims: Their Religious Beliefs and Practices (2nd ed.). Routledge. ISBN 978-0-415-21781-1.

Sachedina, Abdulaziz (1998). The Just Ruler in Shi'ite Islam: The Comprehensive Authority of the Jurist in Imamite Jurisprudence. Oxford University Press US. ISBN 0-19-511915-0.

Smith, Jane I. (2006). The Islamic Understanding of Death and Resurrection. Oxford University Press. ISBN 978-0-19-515649-2.

Teece, Geoff (2003). Religion in Focus: Islam. Franklin Watts Ltd. ISBN 978-0-7496-4796-4.

Trimingham, John Spencer (1998). The Sufi Orders in Islam. Oxford University Press. ISBN

0-19-512058-2.

Turner, Colin (2006). Islam: the Basics. Routledge (UK). ISBN 0-415-34106-X.

Turner, Bryan S. (1998). Weber and Islam. Routledge (UK). ISBN 0-415-17458-9.

Waines, David (2003). An Introduction to Islam. Cambridge University Press. ISBN 0-521-53906-4.

Watt, W. Montgomery (1973). The Formative Period of Islamic Thought. University Press Edinburgh. ISBN 0-85224-245-X.

Watt, W. Montgomery (1974). Muhammad: Prophet and Statesman (New ed.). Oxford University Press. ISBN 0-19-881078-4.

Weiss, Bernard G. (2002). Studies in Islamic Legal Theory. Boston: Brill Academic publishers. ISBN 90-04-12066-1.

Free Books by Charles River Editors

We have brand new titles available for free most days of the week. To see which of our titles are currently free, click on this link.

Discounted Books by Charles River Editors

We have titles at a discount price of just 99 cents everyday. To see which of our titles are currently 99 cents, click on this link.

Made in the USA
Coppell, TX
09 February 2022

73243123R00033